# Helping People with a
# Learning Disability Explore Choice

PO 24228

of related interest

*Helping People with a Learning Disability Explore Relationships*
Eve and Neil Jackson
ISBN 1 85302 688 3

*Learning Disability in Focus*
*The Use of Photography in the Care of People with a Learning Disability*
Eve and Neil Jackson
ISBN 1 85302 693 X

*People Skills for Young Adults*
Márianna Csóti
ISBN 1 85302 716 2

*Lifemaps of People with Learning Disabilities*
Barry Gray and Geoff Ridden
ISBN 1 85302 690 5

*Women with Intellectual Disabilities*
*Finding a Place in the World*
Edited by Rannveig Traustadottir and Kelley Johnson
ISBN 1 85302 846 0

# Helping People with a Learning Disability Explore Choice

*Eve and Neil Jackson*

*Illustrated by Tim Baker*

Jessica Kingsley Publishers
London and Philadelphia

The right of Eve and Neil Jackson to be identified as author of this work has been asserted by them in accordance with the Copyright, Designs and Patents Act 1988.

First published in the United Kingdom in 1999 by
Jessica Kingsley Publishers Ltd
116 Pentonville Road
London N1 9JB, England
and
325 Chestnut Street, Philadelphia
PA 19106, USA.
www.jkp.com

Second edition 2002

Copyright © 1999 Eve and Neil Jackson
Illustrations copyright © 1999 Tim Baker

**Library of Congress Cataloging in Publication Data**
A CIP catalog record for this book is available from the Library of Congress

**British Library Cataloguing in Publication Data**
Jackson, Eve
Helping people with a learning disability explore choice
1. Learning disabled – social conditions
2. Learning disabled – Life skills guides
I. Title II. Jackson, Neil III. Baker, Tim
362.3'86

ISBN 1-85302-694-8

Printed and Bound in Great Britain by
Athenaeum Press, Gateshead, Tyne and Wear

# Contents

# Introduction

The aim of this book is to help people with a learning disability, and those in supportive roles, to work together in developing the skills necessary to make informed choices.

Included in the text are some elements of choice- making and examples of interventions which will help to illustrate the skills required, and some of the errors which are often made.

The book will assist the reader to identify areas where choice is restricted, and demonstrate how to incorporate choice-making into everyday situations. It also underlines the need to be aware of the 'wrong approach', which is often bound up with the carer's attitude.

The book can be used in a range of ways:

- as an easy reader for an adult with learning disabilities

- as a teaching aid for carers and clients to use together in exploring the possibilities of choice-making

- as subject matter to facilitate client and carer workshops, group work or drama sessions.

## Chapter 1

# Moving out

This story is about five people who are going to share a house together.

This is John.

He's already met the people with whom he is going to share the new house.

**John**

There is Terry, who lives with his mum; Danny, who lives with lots of other people; Liz, who lives with her foster mum and dad, her brothers and sisters and the dog; and Lucy, who lives with two elderly ladies.

John lives at Lilac Tree Children's Home. John doesn't really want to move. He has lived at the children's home for nearly seven years and he likes it there. But the decision has been made for him. He has no choice.

'You are sixteen now, John.'

'You're not a small boy any more.'

'You can't live here for ever.'

'You'll soon make new friends.'

John slams doors and tips over rubbish bins. He can't always tell people what he wants or how he feels: he just gets angry.

Terry loves his mum, but he wants to move out. He doesn't want his mum doing everything for him. He has to remind her, 'I'm grown up now, mum. I'm a man'. He wants to learn how to cook and do things for himself. He still wants to visit his mum.

His mum said, 'I will 'phone you every Sunday'.

**Terry**

**Danny**

Danny is fed up with living with so many people who borrow his books and play his tapes. He can't even make himself a cup of tea in peace. He wants to be by himself when he comes in from work – by himself, in his own room. Danny doesn't like lots of people around him.

Liz knows she can't stay with her foster family for ever. She is excited about moving, especially as the new house has a big garden. Liz is going to grow lots of flowers. She will miss her dog, Robo; but she has told Richard, her foster dad, 'I will buy my own dog one

**Liz**

day'. Liz always wants to do lots of things —
usually all at once.

Lucy has lived with Mrs Cole and Miss
James for nearly a year. They are her friends
and she enjoys doing jobs for them. Mrs Cole
always says, 'She's got young legs... not like
us!' But both ladies are going to move into a
flat. A warden will look after them, and do
their shopping for them.

Lucy doesn't want to live by herself. She
likes being with other people... and she likes
telling them what to do! And so Mike said to
her, 'It could be fun living with younger

**Lucy**

people. Why don't you give it a try?' So that's what she is doing.

Mike works for Social Services and Clare works for a housing association. They are going to help John, Terry, Danny, Liz and Lucy to move into their new house at

**5, Wilton Place,**
**Denham,**
**Chineham**
**SF11 4VO.**

They all agree that moving into a new house is exciting. But it will also be a bit scary. 'So many new things to learn!' 'A different routine

**Mike**

**Clare**

to get used to.' They know that living with other people can be difficult.

Now Mike and Clare are already asking then to 'make decisions about the new house' and 'decide how you want to live'. It is a big responsibility – too big! There has been a lot to learn first. Up until now, other people – family, friends, staff – have made even the smallest of choices for them. Up until now, other people have made all the big decisions as well: 'No Terry, wear *that* shirt. I like that one best.'

'It's not the sort of place you'd like at all, Danny.'

'Oh John, don't eat them. You won't like them.'

And people haven't always listened to them. It makes them feel pretty useless... or even angry.

'But I've already *told* you, I'm sorry, but I don't want to go to the shop.'

'Well there's no need to shout, Liz.'

But Mike and Clare know all this. They know that there is a lot to learn. Changes to get used to. It will take time.

Clare and Mike are learning too. They are learning about John, Terry, Danny, Liz and Lucy, getting to know what they like and dislike, what pleases them and what makes them unhappy. They are learning to find out how best to help them.

Clare has already begun to ask questions such as:

'What would you like to do at the weekend?'

'What is your favourite dinner?'

'What kind of clothes do you like best?'

But even that doesn't help much. Because:


If you've always done the same thing every
    weekend,
And you don't know what clubs there are,
Or which places you can visit,
And you don't even know what 'entertainment'
    means;
Then how can you choose?


And if you've always been given the same dinners,
And you haven't tried any new tastes,
And you've never been shown how to cook,
And you don't even know what a 'take-away' is,
Then how can you choose?

And if someone always buys your clothes for you,
And you've got used to wearing them,
And you haven't got any money of your own,
And you don't even know what 'latest fashion'
   means,
Then how can you choose?

**What does 'latest fashion' mean?**

First, John, Terry, Danny, Liz and Lucy will have to get to know *themselves* better. They will have to discover what *they* want:

'I think I'll try that new pub that opened at the weekend.'

What *they* like:

'If I pick any recipe from this cookery book, will you help me to cook it?'

What *they* prefer:

'I think I'll spend the whole day shopping. Then I can try on lots of different clothes.'

Mike and Clare both agree: 'We must keep reminding ourselves that learning how to make informed choices can be difficult.'

'And it takes time to learn', says Clare.

'But it will get easier', adds Mike.

Everyone says, 'Good!' because they all still want to learn.

**They all went to see the house**

## Chapter 2

# Which room is mine?

'It's a big house,' said Lucy.

'It needs to be,' said Clare. 'There are five of you.'

'And you,' said Liz. 'Oh! I nearly forgot! And me.'

'Can we go in?' asked Terry.

'Who's remembered their door key?' asked Mike. They all looked at each other. 'No-one?'

But Danny had. He stepped forward and opened the front door. 'It's empty!' said Terry.

'It echoes,' said Lucy.

'The new furniture will be here by the end of the month,' said Mike.

They explored their new house. John opened every door, even the cupboard doors. Danny looked out of each window. Terry liked the bathrooms best. He turned each tap on and off, and smiled at himself in the mirrors.

Mike and Clare asked Lucy and Liz to each choose a bedroom. The two girls ran upstairs to choose the best room first.

'Is there a room that you like more than the others?' Mike asked Danny.

'Yeah,' said Danny, 'the big one at the end. I've got lots of music and magazines. I need a big room.'

'Good,' said Mike, 'that's a good choice. What about you John?'

John sat on the floor in the middle of a room.

'He likes this one!' shouted Liz.

'This one?' asked Mike. John smiled. 'Yes please!'

**You can see the bus stop from here**

Terry couldn't make up his mind. 'You can't sleep in the bath!' joked Lucy.

Lucy and Liz both wanted the same room. Lucy wanted it because she could see the street and bus stop from the window. She liked watching people. But Liz said she wanted it for the same reason.

'I said it first,' said Lucy.

'And I want to see the bus stop too,' said Liz. 'Pleeease Clare!'

'It's not up to me,' said Clare. 'You and Lucy must work it out between you.'

Lucy stomped out of the room. 'Oh have it then. I don't care. This room's much nicer anyway.' Liz just smiled.

Terry said, 'Can I choose this one?'

'Well, it's not really a choice,' said Clare. 'It's the only one left!'

'But I do like it,' said Terry. 'Come and have a look at *my* room, everyone. It's *mine!*'

Next, they all went out to look at the garden. The grass was very long. They tried to find the path. After a while, Mike asked: 'Where's Liz? She likes gardens.'

Clare and Lucy went to look for her. Liz was still in her new bedroom. But she was crying.

'What's wrong?' asked Clare.

'Is it my room for ever?' sobbed Liz.

'Yes,' said Clare.

'Really?' cried Liz. 'For ever and ever?'

'Yes, it really is yours,' smiled Clare. 'So you can stop worrying.'

But Liz only cried more.

'You can see the bus stop,' said Lucy, trying to cheer her up. But Liz just cried even louder.

Lucy put her arm around her. She thought it was her fault. 'I'm sorry for shouting at you,' she said.

At last Liz stopped crying, and she told them what was wrong: 'I can't see the garden from here. I won't be able to see my flowers in the summer.'

'Do you want to swap with me?' asked Lucy. 'You can see the back garden from my bedroom.'

Liz looked at her in surprise. 'Am I allowed to change my mind?'

'Of course you are,' said Clare. 'I didn't give you a chance to choose. I should have given you more time to think about it. We should have talked it through.'

'You are kind, Lucy,' said Liz. 'And you're my best friend!'

---

*Choice issues: see page 79*

---

## Chapter 3
# Which colour?

Everyone sat in the garden and looked up at the house.

They all agreed that the house was perfect.

'I want to move in now!' said John.

'You will have to wait until it's been painted and decorated,' said Mike.

John closed his eyes. He looked cross. He didn't want to wait.

Clare said: 'Once you've chosen the paint or wallpaper for your rooms, we can get on with the decorating.'

'I don't want paint,' said John.

Liz wanted poppies on her wallpaper. And blue curtains.

Danny wanted two walls dark blue, and two walls white. 'I want to paint my own room,' he said.

Terry wanted someone to help him choose. He 'phoned his mum, who told him 'a creamy colour is best dear...' But John said, 'Have red walls' and Danny said, 'Paint them dark blue, like mine'. Terry wasn't sure what red or blue walls would look like.

Mike said: 'Terry will choose his own colour, thank you.'

**Don't you want to decorate?**

Clare offered to take Lucy shopping to help her choose. But whenever Clare called to take Lucy shopping, she had a new excuse. 'I'm busy today.'

'Don't you want to decorate your new room?' asked Clare.

Lucy said nothing.

'Have you any ideas about how you want to decorate it?' asked Clare. 'It will look so different once it's been decorated.'

Lucy didn't answer. Instead, she talked about the trousers that Clare was wearing. 'Are they new? Where did you buy them?'

'Lucy!' said Clare. 'We are talking about decorating your new room.'

Lucy moved closer and whispered in Clare's ear. 'Clare, I don't know what decorating means.'

'Oh Lucy, I'm so sorry,' said Clare. 'I haven't even explained to you what I mean.'

Once Clare had told Lucy what decorating meant, Lucy couldn't wait to go shopping. She found it easy! Pink wallpaper, posters, a long mirror, more posters…

*Choice issues: see page 82*

## Chapter 4

# Which wallpaper?

Mike went with John and Terry to the DIY shop.

There was loud music playing and John sang along.

'I'll push the trolley,' said John.

Terry looked at the rows and rows of wallpaper. He walked up one row and down the next. He picked up one roll of wallpaper and then put it down. Then he picked up another. There were too many to choose from.

Mike could see that he needed some help.

'Are you sure you want wallpaper and not painted walls?' he asked.

'Yes,' said Terry. He was sure of that.

Mike showed him where the bedroom wallpaper was.

'Do you want flowers, pictures or patterns?' asked Mike, pointing at the rolls of paper.

'Pictures,' said Terry.

'These pictures are for young babies!' said Mike.

Terry picked up a roll of wallpaper. 'For girls! Yuk!'

He threw it back down.

'This is where you need to look,' Mike explained.

'I want this one with football,' said Terry. 'I love football!'

'There are two more with football on them,' said Mike. 'Don't have the first one you see. Take your time.'

Mike got them out so that Terry could see them better.

'This one,' said Terry, and he took one roll of paper from Mike.

'Why that one?' Mike asked.

'The pictures are bigger – and there is a goal!' said Terry.

He took four more rolls from the shelf and went to show them to John.

John was still singing along to the music. But when he saw Mike he began throwing rolls of wallpaper into the trolley.

'But John, that paper has got cars on it. You wanted motorbikes,' said Mike.

'I want this,' said John. 'Can we go now? Can we have dinner? I want chips.'

'Wait, John, are you sure you want that wallpaper?'

But John was already getting money out of his pocket to pay at the cash desk.

Mike, John and Terry went to the Cosy Cafe. John was very, very hungry. He ate a huge

But John, that paper has got cars on it

plate of sausages, chips and beans. When he'd finished eating, he saw the bag with his wallpaper in it. He shoved it with his foot.

'You'll make it dirty,' Terry said. Then John kicked the bag hard.

'John,' said Mike, 'what's wrong?'

John shut his eyes. This time he kicked Terry's chair.

'Stop it!' shouted Terry. People in the cafe looked at them.

'Do you want something else to eat?' asked Mike.

'NO!'

'Do you want to go home?'

'NO!'

John tipped the wallpaper out of the bag. The wallpaper rolled across the floor of the cafe. Terry chased after it.

'Don't you like that wallpaper, John?' asked Mike.

'NO!'

'Then, what do you want to do with it?'

'Give it back,' said John.

'Have you still got the receipt?' Mike asked him. John looked in his pockets.

'Try your wallet,' suggested Terry.

'It's not there,' cried John. He looked on the table and under the plates. Then they all looked on the floor. John crawled under the table. Terry looked in the bag.

'Oh dear,' said Mike. 'They may not let you change the wallpaper without a receipt.'

John rocked his chair. Clack! Clack! Clack! He was getting very angry.

'But I suppose we could try,' Mike added. 'Come on. Let's go back to the shop.'

John didn't want to walk with them. He dragged the bag behind him and mumbled to himself. Then, suddenly, he dropped the bag, ran up to Terry and pushed him.

'Oi!' shouted Terry. 'Don't do that!'

But John grabbed hold of Terry's leg and pulled at his shoe.

'Let go of him!' Mike shouted.

Terry tried to push John away. But John pulled off Terry's shoe and waved it in the air.

'Give me back my shoe!' cried Terry.

'I've got it! I've got it!' John shouted happily. He was waving the till receipt in the air. 'It was on your shoe!'

Terry and Mike laughed.

In the shop this time, John looked at *all* the bedroom wallpapers with pictures on them. He chose some paper with motorbikes on it.

'Are you sure that's the wallpaper you want?' Terry asked him.

'Yes!' said John. 'I can fall asleep dreaming of riding a motorbike. A Harley!'

Choice issues: see page 83

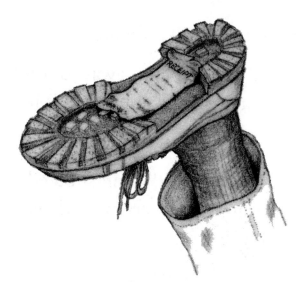

It was on your shoe

## Chapter 5

# Whose job is that?

The new house was soon painted and decorated. Carpets and furniture arrived. Then John, Terry, Danny, Lucy and Liz moved in.

Pictures were hung. Shelves were fixed. Favourite mugs and rugs were put out.

On Friday, Clare called a house meeting. 'We will need some house rules,' she said, 'so that we don't argue over silly things.'

'We had house rules at the Home,' grumbled John. 'Can't do this. Can't do that. All the time.'

'These house rules will make it easier for us all to live together,' said Clare. 'Can you each think of a house rule that will help us? We will talk about them at next week's meeting.'

'What else is there to do?' Lucy asked.

'Jobs,' said Terry.

'No! Not *jobs*!' said John.

'I'll do the hoovering and shopping and make the beds and…'

'Oooh! Wait a minute, Lucy!' cried Clare. 'Give the others a chance!'

'I can look after my own bedroom, thank you,' said Danny. 'No-one is allowed in my room.'

'You can clean the kitchen, Danny,' said Lucy, 'because you're *always* making cups of tea!'

'Stop being bossy,' said Liz, crossly.

'I work hard all day,' said Danny. 'I don't get home until half-past five. I'm too tired to do jobs here as well.'

'It's got to be fair,' said Terry.

'That's right,' said Clare. 'You are all busy during the week. Do you think we will need to pay someone? Just to help us sometimes?'

'Yeah!'

'Good – no jobs then!' said John.

'Oh yes. There will be some,' Clare said. 'We must each be responsible for keeping the house nice.'

'And for looking after ourselves,' added Liz.

John got up and left the room.

'He doesn't want a job,' said Liz.

'Well, John has never had to do any jobs before now,' said Clare. 'We will need to show him how to do them.'

'He can help me,' said Liz. 'I'll polish and dust.'

Just then, there was a loud CRASH! in the kitchen. John had tipped over the bin, and milk was splashed right across the floor.

'He can clean that up,' said Lucy.

'It's not *my* job. *I'm* not doing it,' said Danny.

John ran to his room.

'Let's carry on with the meeting,' said Clare.

Danny was excited. 'I'll help to cook the dinner on Saturday and Sunday. And I'll cut the grass in the summer.'

'I want to do the garden too,' Liz said quickly. 'I want to grow more flowers.'

'I'm doing the shopping,' said Lucy. 'You can come as well Liz – I'll show you how to do it.'

'Can I buy a dog?' asked Liz.

'Mmmm… dog and chips!' laughed Danny.

'And peas!' Terry added.

'That's horrible. I like dogs,' said Liz.

'I don't,' Terry said.

'I'll hoover, if no-one else wants to do it,' said Clare. 'What job do you want to do, Terry?'

Lucy read out a long list of jobs he could do: put away the shopping, wash up, sweep the kitchen floor, empty the bins, clean the bathroom... But there were too many jobs for Terry to choose from.

'Would it help if I gave you two to choose from?' Clare asked him.

Terry nodded.

**Lucy read out a long list**

'Well, you are very good at remembering to do things,' said Clare. 'So, could you choose between emptying the bins every day or cleaning the sinks every day?'

Terry didn't like getting his hands dirty, but he did like the bathrooms. 'Clean the sinks,' he said, smiling.

'What job is John going to do?' Lucy wanted to know. 'It's not fair if he doesn't have a job.'

'I think John needs more time to choose,' Clare replied.

'But if Danny didn't cook the dinner, he'd be hungry,' Terry pointed out.

'And if I didn't get the shopping, we would all starve,' said Lucy.

'I'm sure John will learn that some jobs have to be done,' said Clare.

'You mean, like clearing up his own mess?' Danny asked.

'Yes,' agreed Clare. 'I'll call him down.' But when she went into the kitchen, the spilt milk was gone. She called up the stairs: 'Thanks for clearing up the mess, John!'

'I haven't done it!' he shouted back.

But someone had…!

Choice issues: see page 85

## Chapter 6

# Whose garden is it?

'Shall we have a day in the garden?' asked Clare.

'It *is* hot,' said Lucy. 'I'm going to sunbathe and listen to my radio and write a letter to Mrs Cole.'

Liz got a spade out of the shed. 'I'm going to dig the garden, ready for planting seeds.'

John wanted to dig the garden as well. Danny said he would cut the grass. Terry was keen to help too.

'We can pull up all the weeds,' Clare told him. So Terry followed her along the path.

But Liz wanted the garden to herself. 'Don't pull up any flowers,' she warned Terry. And every time John got ready to dig the garden,

Liz ran across and shouted: 'You can't dig there. I'm planting flowers there.'

Danny could see that John was getting cross.

'You must share the garden, Liz,' said Danny. 'We all like the garden.'

Clare came across to help. 'You should each have your own garden plot. A place to sow your seeds. One for your flowers, Liz. And one for your vegetables, John.'

John stood up on a mound of earth. 'Here,' he said. But Liz said 'Here,' pointing at the same mound of earth.

'Will your seeds grow there?' Clare asked them. 'Or will they grow better over here?'

Clare walked from one side of the garden to the other. She began to think out loud. 'Now, if I plant flowers here, that big tree will shade them. But if I plant them over there, I won't be able to see them from the house.'

She stopped to see if Liz and John were listening.

**Liz and John stood on
the same mound of earth**

'If I plant vegetables too close to that bush, the slugs and snails will eat them...' Clare carried on walking and talking and thinking out loud.

She wondered out loud why some plots were good for growing seeds, and why others were not so good. She was hoping that this might help John and Liz think about why they had chosen their plot. She also hoped it would help them to think about what flowers and vegetables need to help them grow.

Soon, Liz began to do the same as Clare. 'If I plant my seeds here, I can water them more easily. And there's no sun under that big tree.'

John didn't want to walk about talking to himself. He said Clare and Liz were 'potty'. He just said 'There,' and pointed to a plot by the back fence – out of Liz's way. As long as he could grow his vegetables, he was happy. He rubbed his hands together. And Clare knew John well enough to know that that meant: 'Brilliant!'

Clare went back to help Terry. He had filled up a whole bucket with weeds. But he didn't look very happy.

'Lots of weeds for you, Clare,' he told her.

'Oh well done. Shall we pull up some more?'

'No,' said Terry. 'I'm going in now.'

'Don't you like gardening?' asked Clare.

'I don't like the sun: it makes me itchy. Look!' And Terry showed Clare his arms. They were red and sore.

'Oh Terry, why did you stay out in the sun?'

'Because you asked me to help you. I like helping you. I pulled up lots of weeds for you. Are you pleased?'

Clare nodded and smiled. She gave Terry some cream to put on his arms, and then she made cold drinks for everyone. Terry then sat under the big tree and watched John and Liz dig the garden. And he watched Clare pull up weeds… by herself.

*Choice issues: see page 87*

Chapter 7

# What's in the garden?

That evening they all looked at gardening magazines. There were pictures of flower gardens and vegetable gardens, Japanese gardens and water gardens.

'What shall we have in our garden?' asked Clare.

'Lots of flowers!' said Liz.

'Carrots and tomatoes!' said John.

'I don't know,' said Lucy. 'I've never had a garden before.'

'A garden seat?' suggested Clare. Everyone said 'Yeah!' to that.

'It was just grass at the Home,' said John. 'But I did grow carrots.'

'A pond, with fish!' said Danny.

'Roses, like my mum's!' said Terry. 'She likes red roses best.'

'Will you make a list of the things that you like best?' Clare asked. 'Or put a tick by them. It will help us to choose.'

'Is there room for a swimming pool?' asked Liz, hopefully.

'No room and no money,' said Clare. 'But maybe a pond, as Danny suggested.'

'A pond is where ducks and swans live,' said Lucy.

'No, ours will be smaller than that,' said Clare quickly. 'A garden pond.'

'What does it look like?' asked Lucy.

'Sort of this shape. Or this shape. Or any shape really,' said Danny, waving his arms.

Lucy felt even more confused.

'Here's a picture of one,' said Terry.

'But it looks like a black hole,' Lucy said.

'I think we had better go to the garden centre, to show you what we mean,' Clare told her.

The afternoon at the garden centre was even more fun than looking at magazines had been. Lucy saw some garden ponds with fish in them, and some with plants in them. John and Liz bought the seeds they needed. Danny looked at the new lawnmowers. Terry and John tried out all the garden furniture.

The next day they drew a plan of the garden. Then they added all the things they wanted to put in it.

Danny laughed. 'There'll be no room for us!'

'It'll be a jungle!' said John, excitedly.

John and Liz planted the seeds they had bought. They watered them and put a marker in the ground beside them. On the marker they wrote: DO NOT WALK ON SEEDS to remind people.

'Don't go near my flower seeds,' Liz warned John.

'Don't want to!' John replied.

John told everybody, 'Mind the seeds!' But in the morning, when John and Liz went to look at the garden, there was a big hole in the flowerbed…

'Right in the middle of my seeds!' cried Liz. 'You did it!' she shouted at John.

'No I didn't, I didn't,' said John.

Liz called to the others. 'Who's done this?' she asked.

They all shook their heads. 'Not me, Liz.'

'Maybe someone came into the garden during the night,' Terry said.

'A burglar!' said Lucy.

'Has anything been taken?' asked Danny. 'Have you looked in the garden shed?'

Liz went to have a look. Then she stopped. 'There's noise in the shed. I think someone's in there.'

No-one wanted to go and look.

'You're the oldest, Danny. *You* look,' said Lucy.

'No!' cried Liz. 'It's dangerous!'

But Danny said, 'No it's not,' and he walked towards the shed. He put his hand on the door handle. There was a loud CRASH!

**Danny swung open the door**

'Come out!' called Danny as he swung open the door.

'Miaow!'

'It's a kitten!'Danny laughed. He picked it up and showed it to everyone. They all said 'Aahh!' and stroked it till it miaowed some more.

'You're a bad kitten!' Liz told it.

'It's hungry,' said Clare. 'Let's find it some milk.'

As the kitten lapped up the milk, John started to laugh.

'What's so funny?' asked Terry.

'The kitten is my friend!' said John. 'I think it cleaned the kitchen floor for me the other night.'

'That's right,' said Liz. '*We* didn't clean up the milk. And *John* didn't. It must have been the kitten!'

'Shall we keep it?' asked Danny.

'Yes!' they all agreed at once. Even Terry liked kittens!

'Who's going to look after it?' Danny wondered.

'I will!' cried John. 'It will be my job. I will make a bed for it. And I will buy cat food.'

'But we can't keep it – it's not ours,' Lucy pointed out.

'Maybe someone has lost it,' said Terry.

'Someone might be looking for it,' said Liz.

'What do you think you should do?' asked Clare.

'I think we should tell the police,' said Danny.

'And the RSPCA!' Liz added.

So they telephoned the police and the RSPCA, and they also decided to put a notice in the shop window. The notice read:

```
┌─────────────────────────────────────┐
│            FOUND                     │
│  BLACK AND WHITE KITTEN              │
│          ADDRESS:                    │
│  5, WILTON PLACE, DENHAM,            │
│    CHINEHAM SFl1 4VO.                │
└─────────────────────────────────────┘
```

John liked looking after the kitten. He had never had a pet of his own. He wanted to keep it.

'Are you coming with us, John?' asked Liz. 'We are going to ask the neighbours if they have lost a kitten.'

'No!' said John. 'It will be lonely by itself.'

Terry, Danny, Lucy, Liz and Clare knocked at every door in Wilton Place.

'My feet are aching,' Lucy complained.

'There is only one house left,' said Clare. 'We will ask there and then go home.'

Clare knocked at the door and asked one last time: 'Have you lost a black and white kitten?'

The lady at the door suddenly smiled. 'Oh yes, yes I have. I thought it had been run over by a car. Oh I'm so glad it's safe.'

'What's its name?' asked Terry.

'Oh, I've got too many to give them all names,' said the lady. 'Come in and have a look.'

There was cat sitting on the back of the chair. Two cats on the window sill. One in the kitchen eating its dinner. Four cats prowling in the garden. And kittens *everywhere.*

'Would you like some tea?' offered the lady.

They stayed for some time. They stroked each cat and played with the kittens.

When they got home they had good news to tell John.

'We found the lady who owns the kitten,' said Liz.

'She's got lots of cats,' said Terry.

'And more kittens!' added Lucy. 'She was pleased that we'd found it. She gave us tea.'

'And cream cakes!' said Liz. "Mmmm!'

But John didn't think it was good news. 'I want to keep it. I wanted to see the other kittens. I didn't know you were going to have cakes. You didn't tell me that, Clare!'

'But John,' said Clare, 'I didn't know that we would be invited to tea. It was unexpected. A surprise.'

John was still grumpy. 'I should have come with you and not stayed here.'

'But we do have a surprise for you as well, John,' smiled Clare.

'What is it?' asked John.

'The lady said she had too many cats and kittens to look after. She said we can keep this one.'

John whooped with joy. He picked up the kitten and kissed it.

'What shall we call it?' Terry wanted to know.

John knew. He had been thinking about it all afternoon. 'Daisy.'

'Why Daisy?' Liz asked him.

'Because if she digs up more of your seeds,' John explained, 'she will be the only flower in the garden!'

**Daisy**

*Choice issues: see page 89*

Chapter 8

# Which person?

Already the new house felt like home. Families and old friends visited John, Danny, Terry, Lucy and Liz, and new friends were made.

**Already the new house felt like home**

They found it fun to try out new things. Visit different places. Learn new skills. It was a way of finding out about themselves, finding out what they *really* liked. Having a choice was important to them now.

So, when Mike and Clare told them, '*We* will be interviewing the five people who have applied for the job,' they were all very disappointed.

'We need someone to help when Clare is away,' explained Mike.

'It is a big decision,' said Clare. 'We must make sure that we choose the right person.'

'But what about us?' cried Lucy. 'We have to choose too – it's our home.'

Mike and Clare looked at each other and thought for a moment. Then Mike said: 'One of you must help us to hold the interviews. And all of you will meet the five people.'

Lucy smiled. 'We'll tell you which person we like best.'

Everyone agreed that Danny should help to interview. When the people who came for the interviews arrived, Lucy and Terry gave them tea. John and Liz showed them the garden while they waited.

Mike and Clare had plenty of questions to ask.

'Why did you leave your last job?'

'What made you apply for this job?'

'Can you work weekends?'

Danny couldn't think of any good questions to ask, but he did listen carefully to what everyone had to say.

Lucy and Terry were very quiet. They just passed the biscuits and smiled a lot. Some of the people asked them questions: they liked that. John and Liz talked a lot about the garden. They asked the people:

'Do you like gardening?'

and

'Have you got a pond?'

and

'Do you like our new garden seat?'

They both liked one man, who talked to Daisy. Daisy miaowed loudly.

But everyone was glad when the day was over.

Mike and Clare said to the people as they left: 'We'll let you know by the end of the week.'

They had a house meeting to talk about the interviews.

'They were all nice,' said Terry.

Mike and Clare explained why some of the people would be no good for the job. 'The first lady didn't want to do housework. She didn't want to climb up and down the stairs all day.'

'One man didn't want to work at the weekends,' Mike said. 'And another lady wasn't sure if the job would suit her.'

'Who did *you* like?' asked Clare. They all looked at each other.

'We liked them all,' said Lucy.

'What about you, Danny?' asked Mike. 'You heard us asking them questions.'

Danny shrugged. 'Can't remember.'

'Liz? John?'

'What did the first lady look like?' Liz asked.

Mike opened an envelope. 'Sorry: I nearly forgot. Maybe these will help you to remember.' He spread out a line of photographs. 'I asked them to bring photos of themselves.'

'Does that help?' asked Clare.

They all smiled. They saw the person they wanted.

'That one,' said John.

**I asked them to bring a
photo of themselves**

'Yes, him!' exclaimed Liz.

'Yes!' Terry and Lucy said together. 'That's him!'

'Mr Stanley! I remember now. I liked him best!' shouted Danny.

They had all chosen the same person. Mr Stanley was their choice.

But Mike and Clare shook their heads. 'No. We can't give him the job,' said Mike. 'He is unreliable.'

'He only stayed in his last job for two months,' Clare explained. 'And he left the job he had before that after only a few weeks.'

'But we want him to work here. We like him,' said Danny. 'We've *all* chosen Mr Stanley.'

Mike and Clare wanted them to choose someone else. They didn't agree with John, Terry, Danny, Liz or Lucy. This was very difficult for them. So at last they said: 'We all need more time to think about it.'

The next day, they held another house meeting. John, Terry, Danny, Liz and Lucy had not changed their minds. They still wanted Mr Stanley to have the job, and they each had a good reason for liking Mr Stanley.

John said: 'He likes cats and gardening. He was gentle with Daisy.'

Terry said: 'He wanted to know all about me. Most people don't want to know.'

Danny said: 'He had good reasons for leaving his other jobs. He told us in the interview. I trust him.'

Liz said: 'He talked to me as if I was a lady and not a little girl.'

Lucy said: 'I think he really really wants the job. And I just like him.'

So Mike and Clare gave in. 'Okay, we'll give Mr Stanley the job for just three months to begin with. That will give him time to see whether he likes the job, and whether we like him.' They all agreed.

Danny telephoned Mr Stanley to tell him. Mr Stanley was very happy. John, Terry, Danny, Liz and Lucy knew that Mike and Clare had listened to them. They hadn't told them who they should like or what they should do.

They had chosen Mr Stanley. They were in control. It made them feel good. They felt like celebrating.

'Let's have a party!' shouted John.

'YEAH!'

**Let's have a party**

*Choice issues: see page 91*

# Questions to ask
# yourself and others

- Why is it important to be able to choose?
- Do you think being able to choose is something that needs to be learnt? Do you need to learn?
- Why do you want to choose for yourself?
- Who usually chooses for you?
- Why do you think other people want to choose for you?
- Is there any risk involved in choosing by yourself?
- How do you feel if someone chooses for you?
- Should you always be able to choose for yourself?

- What happens if someone disagrees with your choice?
- Does anything stop you from choosing sometimes?
- How can someone make it easier for you to choose?
- Do you ever choose something in order to please someone else?
- Have you ever regretted choosing something?
- Why might it be difficult for family, friends or carers when you first begin to choose for yourself?
- Do you think you do some things out of habit rather than choice?
- Have you ever chosen something and then changed your mind? Did it matter?
- To be able to choose, you need to know what you like. How will you find out what you like?

- Do you always experience a 'result' from choosing something? In other words, does something have to 'happen'?
- How does choosing make you feel?

# Choice issues

## Chapter 2: Which room is mine?

- Self-concept or self-picture
- Feedback
- Awareness of preferences
- Consequences
- Regrets
- Illusion of choice

*Suggestions of how to put choice-making into practice, with illustrations from the story-line*

1. Having a **self-concept** or **self-picture** is a pre-requisite for making a choice. A *self-concept* or *picture* will enable a person to identify and articulate their needs and thereby gain new life experiences.

   Example: Danny understood what his needs were: 'I've got lots of music and magazines. I need a big room.'

2. Always offer **positive feedback** when a choice is made. This will help the person making a choice by reinforcing their actions.

> Example: 'Good…that's a good choice.'

3. In order to develop someone's **awareness of preferences,** it will be necessary to offer him or her increased opportunities and *experiences.*

> Example: Liz had already experienced the enjoyment of growing flowers and planned to do it again. 'I won't be able to see my flowers in the summer.'

4. The long-term **consequences** of a choice made can be understood more fully if you talk it through carefully. Always give time appropriate to the person's abilities.

> Example: 'I didn't give you much time to choose. I should have given you more time to think about it. We should have talked it through.'

5. **Regrets** and other *thoughts* and *feelings* can be *explored* and *acknowledged* if discussed at an appropriate time. A change of mind needs to be seen as part of the learning process and should be accepted as normal behaviour. (We all do it!)

> Example: 'Am I allowed to change my mind?'

Choices with *long-term consequences* often have to be *re-evaluated* in the light of change – and our inability to predict the future.

6. Try to avoid giving the **illusion of choice.** This will confuse and set back learning. It is also dishonest.

> Example: Clare acted with honesty by telling Terry: 'Well, it's not really a choice... it's the only one left!'

# Chapter 3: Which colour?

- New concepts
- Making assumptions
- Exploring alternative options

*Suggestions of how to put choice-making into practice, with illustrations from the story-line*

1. After a **new concept** has been introduced, check that it has been correctly understood. It takes time to understand new meanings and ideas, and they will need to be given in context and repeated often.

   Example: 'It will look so different once it's been decorated.'

   This can easily lead to **wrong assumptions** being made.

   Example: 'Don't you want to decorate your new room?'

2. You will need to be imaginative when helping someone to **explore alternative options.** Use all of the person's *senses,* if appropriate. Show or give examples of what you mean. Offer suggestions.

   Example: Terry would have benefited from seeing some paint: 'Terry wasn't sure what red or blue walls would look like.'

# Chapter 4: Which wallpaper?

- Conflicting stimuli
- Too much choice
- Attention span
- Checking thoughts and reasons
- Conflicting needs
- After-event feelings

*Suggestions of how to put choice-making into practice, with illustrations from the story-line*

1. Try to be aware of any **conflicting stimuli** that could disturb a person's concentration. Maybe remind or prompt occasionally to keep him or her *on task.*

   Example: John appeared to enjoy the music more than shopping. 'John was still singing along to the music.'

2. Sometimes **too much choice** can be confusing.

   Example: 'Terry looked at the rows and rows of wallpaper.'

   By organising the way a choice is presented, such as breaking it into smaller steps, you will make it manageable and more accessible.

   Example: 'Do you want flowers, pictures or patterns?'

3. If someone's **attention span** is known to be limited, you will find that planning ahead will prove invaluable. In the story, Mike had difficulty sharing equal time and attention between John and Terry.

4. By **checking** the **thoughts and reasons** behind a choice, you can *assess learning* and give clarification or feedback as appropriate.

    Example: '"Why that one?" Mike asked.'

5. Do take into account the possibility of **conflicting needs.** A person's response may be contingent on how he or she feels at that particular time.

    Example: 'John was very, very hungry.'

6. You may find that **after-event feelings,** such as *regret,* may be expressed inappropriately.

    Example: 'John rocked his chair.'

It may be useful to *observe* and *record* responses in different situations. These may then be *shaped* and *reinforced* by the carer over time. Accurate observation allows you to see what the person is really saying.

# Chapter 5: Whose job is that?

- Shared activities
- Limiting choice
- Accepting responsibility
- Past experiences
- Legitimate response

*Suggestions of how to put choice-making into practice, with illustrations from the story-line*

1. **Shared activities** such as house meetings can help in the development of interpersonal skills and the building of confidence. People should be encouraged to verbalise their own needs and wishes and to participate fully in order to maximise the control they have over their lives.

   Example: 'Clare called a house meeting…"Can you each think of a house rule…?"'

2. **Limiting a person's choice** may be used as a stage in the learning process. This can avoid frustration, and even embarrassment.

   Example: Terry was having difficulty making a decision, so Clare asked him: 'Would it help if I gave you two to choose from?'

   But it should *never* be used as an alternative to developing someone's skills further, or as an excuse not to do so.

3. Making choices is part of **accepting responsibilities,** but it may take time for a person to fully appreciate that it is sometimes inevitable that a choice must be made. It may help to demonstrate what is required as well as offering a clear explanation.

> Example: 'We will need to show him... I think John needs more time to choose.'

But do remember that *not all choice-making can be based on past experiences.* The unknown can be frightening.

4. To able to appreciate why someone is reluctant to be involved in an activity such as choice-making, **past experiences** may need to be explored and understood.

> Example: 'We had house rules... Can't do this. Can't do that.'

5. Absenting oneself, or refusing to comply with a request, should be recognised as **legitimate responses** and areas where further learning can take place.

> Example: 'John got up and left the room.'

See point 6 on page 84 for further suggestions.

# Chapter 6: Whose garden is it?

- Making an assumption
- Willingness to please
- Thinking out loud
- Understanding responses

*Suggestions of how to put choice-making into practice, with illustrations from the story-line*

1. It is any easy mistake to **make an assumption** that you know what a person likes or wants. Sometimes it comes about out of habit, or over-familiarity. Try taking 'time out' to *reflect* on whether it is your own wishes and desires that are being granted.

   Example: Clare wanted to clear the weeds and took it for granted that Terry would help: 'Terry followed Clare.'

2. Be aware how **willing to please** some people may be. Try posing the question differently or offer an alternative, and do be conscious of your own *non-verbal behaviour* throughout – we all know the power of a pitiful look!

   Example: Terry's willingness to please superseded his own comfort. 'You asked me to help you. I like helping you... Are you pleased?'

3. **Thinking out loud** and encouraging a client to do the same will allow for some *exploration into the logic* behind a decision. It will also prompt him or her to *make use of knowledge gained previously.*

> Example: 'Clare carried on walking and talking... Soon Liz began to do the same as Clare. 'If I plant my seeds here...'

4. Not enough emphasis can be put on 'getting to know' the person in order to **understand their response.** Observe and record if necessary.

> Example: 'John rubbed his hands together. And Clare knew John well enough to know that that meant: "Brilliant!"'

# Chapter 7: What's in the garden?

- Evaluation and refining your own skills
- Learned helplessness
- Motivation
- Complementary skill
- Unpredicted outcomes

*Suggestions of how to put choice-making into practice, with illustrations from the story-line*

1. An essential part of looking at different ways of presenting facts is being prepared to **evaluate and refine your own skills,** as part of your own on-going learning. Maybe ask yourself: What other skills or knowledge do I need to help this person to understand? Do I need to discuss it with others? Brainstorm ideas? Break it into smaller steps?

   > Example: Clare thought that looking in magazines would give Lucy adequate information about gardens, but then had to think it through again. '[We'll] go to the garden centre, to show you what we mean.'

2. If someone rarely experiences the outcome of a choice he or she has made, that person may come to believe that he or she has no influence over events in his or her life. This is often termed **'a learned helplessness'.**

For some people discovering the **motivation** to choose will be the first step towards choice making. Try and make it a positive experience for the person. One they will remember and want to repeat.

> Example: John really wanted a pet of his own. 'It will be my job. I will make a bed for it. And I will buy cat food.'

3. **Complementary skills** can be learnt through shared activities, when discussion and problem-solving can take place. These situations should be initiated whenever possible.

> Example: Clare encouraged everyone to participate in planning the garden. 'That evening they all looked at gardening magazines.' But she took a 'back seat' when they were discussing the kitten – 'What do you think you should do?'

4. Unfortunately, some **outcomes** are **unpredicted**. Disappointment and regret may need to be worked through. It is all part of the person's development.

> Example: John was confused: 'I didn't know you were going to have cakes. You didn't tell me... I should have come with you.'

# Chapter 8: Which person?

- Increasing opportunities
- Risk taking
- Evaluation
- Opportunity to practice
- Visual cues

*Suggestions of how to put choice-making into practice, with illustrations from the story-line*

1. A person will only be able to move *towards autonomy* if he or she is engaged in **more choice-making opportunities** in line with growing confidence and increased abilities.

   Example: 'Having a choice was important to them now... 'We have to choose too – it's our home.'

2. Inevitably, sooner or later **risk-taking** will have to be acknowledged. It will mean being creative in finding *strategies to minimise the risk* involved and avoid failure. One way may be to set short-term objectives that can be evaluated often.

   Example: Clare and Mike were aware of the risk involved in including the others in the interviewing process – 'it's a big decision'. They decided that offering a short-term contract to Mr Stanley was appropriate – 'for just three months to begin with'.

3. Preparing someone for a new situation is necessary if that person is to function well. Giving the person the **opportunity to practise** in a *role-play* situation allows them to feel, experience and experiment in a safe/non-threatening environment.

> Example: Had Mike and Clare run through a role-play with Danny before they started interviewing, Danny would have been able to prepare relevant questions – 'Danny couldn't think of any good questions to ask'.

4. A camera can be one of the most useful *aids to offering choice*. It allows you to give a clear **visual cue** when presenting options, and is particularly useful when reminders of past experiences and events are required.

> Example: 'He spread out a line of photos... "I remember him now."'

# Glossary of terms used

**Accepting responsibility** Accepting accountability for your actions and the consequences of those actions.

**After-event feelings** Emotional responses that are experienced after a choice has been made; may be positive or negative.

**Aids to offering choice** Use of cues, actual objects or photographs of objects, people and places, that will act as reminders and facilitate the making of an informed choice.

**Attention span** Time that a person can stay focused on a task, activity or source of stimulation.

**Autonomy** Individual freedom, personal space and control over one's environment and life.

**Back seat** Allowing others to take the initiative in discussions and problem-solving.

**Complementary skills** Skills that will enhance the process of choice-making.

**Conflicting needs** The gratification of one need obstructing the gratification of another.

**Conflicting stimuli** More than one source of stimulation, resulting in an inability to focus on a task or activity.

**Consequences** Outcomes of a decision or choice, they may be planned or unplanned, positive or negative.

**Contingent** Dependency on something to occur or be present before something else can happen; in other words, choices have to be made available before a choice can be made.

**Cues** Things that remind us to do something; for example, an alarm clock, notes in our diary, notes on the fridge door, reminders given by other people.

**Evaluate** The act of examining and judging the worth and significance of your own knowledge and learning.

**Explore alternative options** To look for other ways of doing something; for example, brainstorming possibilities.

**Explore the logic behind the decision** To test the validity of a potential choice or decision. Is it sensible, can it be achieved?

**Feedback** Reflecting back progress made and giving encouragement, this may lead to actions being changed or developed.

**Illusion of choice** Offering choice that is not viable or within the sphere of authority of the offerer, suggesting there is a choice when in fact there is not.

**Increasing opportunities** Broadening the experiences that people have by exposing them to different situations and relationships in which they can explore choices and options.

**Learned helplessness** The inability to make a choice as a consequence of having had no previous influence over events or decision-making.

**Legitimate response** Feelings related to a potential choice which can be expressed through verbal, non-verbal or behavioural action. The behaviour may be socially in-appropriate, but it is still valid.

**Limiting choice** Deliberately not offering a full range of options in the knowledge that the person would be unable to assimilate that amount of information.

**Making assumptions** Assuming knowledge, ability or preferences.

**Motivation** The interest or desire that stimulates someone to make a choice.

**New concepts** Any experience that someone has previously lacked. Also, language with which the person is not familiar.

**Non-verbal behaviour** The expression of what you feel and believe through the way language or physical actions are used. It is possible to say we agree with something and yet to indicate that we do not by facial expression, tone of voice, or other non-verbal means.

**Observing and recording responses** Noting behaviour in order to discover meaning through understanding the context in which it occurs. Careful records must be kept in order to build up an accurate picture of the client.

**On task** Carrying out an activity through to its conclusion without being distracted.

**Preferences** The knowledge that one thing is liked more than another.

**Recognising and acknowledging achievement** Pro-viding focused feedback by acknowledging specific achievements, thereby avoiding meaningless positive statements — for example, remarking 'you washed those cups well' would be more accurate than just saying 'well done'.

**Regret** Acknowledgment that people will make decisions that they regret and that this is part of the learning process.

**Reinforcing** Using accurate positive feedback to increase the likelihood that the behaviour will occur again, as, 'you washed those cups well'.

**Risk-taking** The use of situations in which there is an element of risk, in order to develop skills and knowledge.

**Role-play** Technique through which a person may learn to function more effectively by trying out new ways of behaving.

**Self-concept or self-picture** A sense of one's identity, needs, preferences and dislikes.

**Shaping** Systematically building a correct response to teach a new behaviour.

**Strategies to minimise risk** Finding ways to reduce the potential for risk, perhaps through formulating a risk-taking policy.

**Unpredicted outcomes** Consequences of a choice that were not planned for.